Chester Carlson and the Development of Xerography

Susan Zannos

Mitchell Lane
PUBLISHERS

Unlocking the Secrets of Science

Profiling 20th Century Achievers in Science, Medicine, and Technology

Chester Carlson and the Development of Xerography

Copyright © 2003 by Mitchell Lane Publishers, Inc. All rights reserved. No part of this book may be reproduced without written permission from the publisher. Printed and bound in the United States of America.

Printing   1   2   3   4   5   6   7   8   9

Library of Congress Cataloging-in-Publication Data
Zannos, Susan.
    Chester Carlson and the development of xerography/Susan Zannos.
        p. cm. — (Unlocking the secrets of science)
    Summary: Traces the life of the man whose determination to simplify the process of copying documents led to the invention of the process of xerography.
    Includes bibliographical references and index.
    ISBN 1-58415-117-X
    1. Carlson, Chester Floyd, 1906-1968—Juvenile literature. 2. Xerography—History—Juvenile literature. [1. Carlson, Chester Floyd, 1906-1968. 2. Inventors. 3. Xerography—History.] I. Title. II. Series.
    TR1045 .Z36 2002
    681'.65'092—dc21
    [B]   2002023658

ABOUT THE AUTHOR: Susan Zannos has been a lifelong educator, having taught at all levels, from preschool to college, in Mexico, Greece, Italy, Russia, and Lithuania, as well as in the United States. She has published a mystery *Trust the Liar* (Walker and Co.) and *Human Types: Essence and the Enneagram* was published by Samuel Weiser in 1997. She has written several books for children, including *Paula Abdul* and *Cesar Chavez* (Mitchell Lane). Susan lives in Oxnard, California.

PHOTO CREDITS: cover: Catherine Carlson; p. 6 Catherine Carlson; p. 11 Xerox; pp. 12, 14, 15, 16 Catherine Carlson; p. 18 Xerox; p. 20 Catherine Carlson; pp. 22, 24, 28, 31, 32, 34, 35, 38, 41, 42, 44, 47, 49, 50 (top) Xerox; p. 50 (bottom) Catherine Carlson

ABOUT THESE PHOTOS: Most of the photographs in this book are very old and have come from the personal collections of both Catherine Carlson and Xerox.

OUR THANKS: To Catherine Carlson for reviewing this story and approving it for print, and for supplying us with photographs.

PUBLISHER'S NOTE: In selecting those persons to be profiled in this series, we first attempted to identify the most notable accomplishments of the 20th century in science, medicine, and technology. When we were done, we noted a serious deficiency in the inclusion of women. For the greater part of the 20th century science, medicine, and technology were male-dominated fields. In many cases, the contributions of women went unrecognized. Women have tried for years to be included in these areas, and in many cases, women worked side by side with men who took credit for their ideas and discoveries. Even as we move forward into the 21st century, we find women still sadly underrepresented. It is not an oversight, therefore, that we profiled mostly male achievers. Information simply does not exist to include a fair selection of women.

Contents

Chester Carlson spent most of his lifetime struggling to invent a workable, inexpensive copy machine. He invented the process of xerography, but that was only the beginning. Though he was never employed by the Haloid Company or Xerox, he was a consultant to them and helped develop the Xerox Model 914, the first plain paper copier.

Chapter 1

Depression

● ●

The year is 1934, at the height of the Great Depression after the economy of the United States collapsed in 1929. The setting is a drab office in the P.R. Mallory electronics firm in New York City. The central figure is a young man hunched over pages of print and drawings that he must laboriously copy by hand and by typewriter. The young man is Chester Carlson, and he is getting very frustrated.

Carlson is working in the company's patent department. A patent is the right to an invention or discovery, and is issued by the Patent and Trademark Office of the United States government. The right is, in the official language, "the right to exclude others from making, using, offering for sale, or selling" the invention in the United States or "importing" the invention into the United States. The term of a new patent is 17 years from the time the application is first filed in the United States. The patents Carlson is working with have to do with various electronic devices to which the P.R. Mallory Company has the rights.

One reason the 28-year-old Carlson is frustrated is that even though he is a physicist, with his college degree from the California Institute of Technology, this job doesn't really utilize his education. Another reason is that his job doesn't pay very much. He only recently got out of debt and it's still hard to get ahead.

But the primary reason he is frustrated is that he wishes he could be working on some of the inventions he has been thinking about. Instead, he is stuck in a job he doesn't like much, where there never seem to be enough copies of the patent applications he has to complete, and copying them day after day is terribly laborious. Because he is nearsighted, he has to bend over to see the papers. This cramps his muscles and gives him a backache.

There has to be a better way to make all these copies than doing them by hand, the young man thinks. If only there were some way to just press a button and get a perfect copy, his life would be a lot easier. In fact, he thinks, if he could invent such a device his life would also be better because other people would want it, too. Then he could sell it, and he would make more money than he is making right now while he copies patents.

There were some methods used for making copies of documents during that time, but none of them were very good because they all had major drawbacks. There was carbon paper, for instance, and Chester used a lot of it. Carbon paper, which was originally created in the early 1800s to help blind people write, is a thin sheet of paper coated with a mixture of wax and pigment. It is put between two sheets of ordinary paper to make one or more copies of an original document. But carbon paper could only be used for outgoing documents. If a copy was needed of an incoming document, it had to be produced by hand.

Furthermore, carbon paper was messy. The "carbon" rubbed off on everything it touched. It couldn't make more than two copies because the typewriter keys, or the pen or pencil, couldn't press hard enough to go through more than five layers—three pieces of typing paper and two of carbon paper—and even then the last copy was often very faint and hard to read. Carbon paper is seldom used now, except for books of receipts where the original is for the customer, the carbon is thrown away, and a copy is left in the book.

Another way of making multiple copies was the mimeograph machine. Thomas Edison invented the mimeograph and transferred the patent to the A.B. Dick Co. of Chicago in 1887 so they could produce it commercially. The "mime" comes from the ancient Greek word mimos, which meant a comic theater. This root word, seen in "mimic" for instance, means to imitate. "Graphein," also Greek, meant writing. So the mimeograph produced "imitation writing," or copies.

The mimeograph machine needed a prepared stencil that could be made in a typewriter or drawn by hand. The stencil was clamped onto a cylinder. As the cylinder was turned, either by hand or electricity, a pressure roller forced sheets of paper against the stencil, which forced mimeograph fluid and ink through the openings cut into the stencil. The mimeograph, or mimeo for short, was widely used in schools to prepare many copies of tests, quizzes, study guides and examinations for use by students.

But the mimeograph method had several drawbacks. The stencils were time-consuming to make, the copies were blurry and hard to read, and they smelled bad. The mimeograph fluid smelled awful. And, as with carbon paper, copies could only be made to give out. There was no way to copy something that had been received.

There were also various photographic methods for copying documents, but these were also messy and took a long time. Basically they required taking a photograph of the document, then developing the photograph in a darkroom. Special papers and chemicals were needed, so these processes were not only time-consuming but expensive as well.

Another common way to make copies in the 1930s was by offset printing. A printer named Ira W. Rubel discovered the offset printing process in 1904. It is based on the fact that water and oil do not mix, so greasy ink can be put on the printing areas of a plate while non-printing areas hold water and reject the ink. The offset printing plate was metal, usually zinc or aluminum, with a specially treated surface that hardened in the printing areas and washed away in the non-printing areas. A special paper master had to be made and then the image transferred to the printing plate. Offset printing produced very good copies, but it took a long time and was expensive.

None of these methods was useful for making the copies of patent applications that Chester Carlson so laboriously produced by hand. What he needed was a device that would make clear, accurate copies of any document or drawing or image, on ordinary paper, without smelly and expensive chemicals, without a long drawn-out process, for only a few cents a copy.

What he needed was a copy machine. Why didn't he use one? Because it hadn't been invented. Chester Carlson was going to invent it. But it was going to be a very long, difficult process. He often became so discouraged that he simply wanted to give up. But inventors are different from most other people. What seems to make them different is that they keep on long after any reasonable person would have quit. That certainly seemed to be the case with Carlson.

Many times he wanted to quit, but he kept on. Eventually he succeeded.

Carlson's life is like a story by the 19th century writer Horatio Alger, a story in which a poor, honest, hard-working boy overcomes tremendous obstacles to become a success. In Chester Carlson's case the financial success exceeded $200 million, but he wasn't particularly interested in money and gave most of it away.

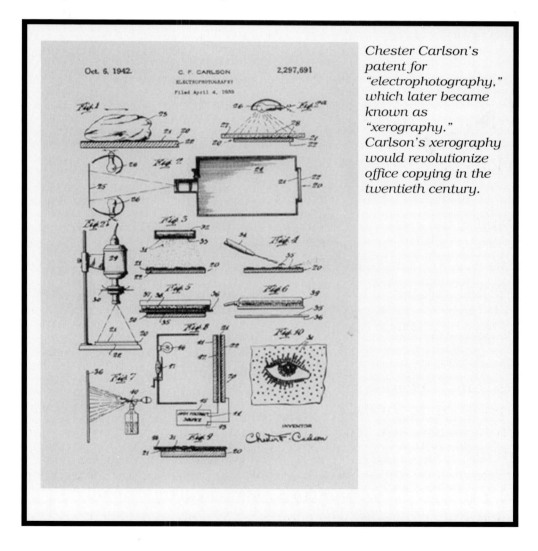

Chester Carlson's patent for "electrophotography," which later became known as "xerography." Carlson's xerography would revolutionize office copying in the twentieth century.

Carlson's graduation photograph when he was 18 years old.

Chapter 2

Early Years

• •

Chester Floyd Carlson was born on February 8, 1906 in Seattle, Washington, to Olaf and Ellen Carlson. His father was a barber, while his mother was a housewife. His parents were descended from Swedish farmers who came to this country and settled in the state of Minnesota. Chester, or Chet as he preferred to be known, was to be their only child because neither of his parents was healthy.

"About a year after I was born my father was brought down with a severe case of tuberculosis," Carlson recalled in later life. "As if that were not enough, he also developed arthritis of the spine, the two together rapidly reduced him to a bent, emaciated wreck of a man who was to spend the greater part of each day for the next 26 years lying flat on his back, wracked by coughing spells and defeated by the world. This, plus the resulting poverty and isolation, was to have a profound effect on my development."

Seattle's chilly, often damp climate wasn't a good place for a man who suffered with these diseases, so Olaf moved the family soon after his son's birth in search of a warmer, sunnier climate in which his health might improve. By the time Chet was six, the family had been in Arizona and Mexico before ending up in a run-down rented farmhouse in San Bernardino, California. But his father's health problems continued to worsen and the boy soon had to work at any job he could find to help support the family. By the time he was 14, his father's arthritis had become so crippling that he could no longer work as a barber, and Chet—a shy, skinny boy—was the family's main financial support.

From the age of 12, Chester contributed a large part to the family income. He raised and sold guinea pigs. This photo was taken in San Bernadino, California in 1918.

He would get up at 5:00 a.m. to wash store windows before he went to school. After school he did janitorial work, sweeping out offices and the local bank. By the time Chet was a junior in high school—which was also the year his mother died of tuberculosis—he was working as a printer's assistant as well as at his janitorial jobs. In his senior year in high school he worked weekends in a chemical laboratory.

Because much of the work was dull and repetitive, Chet's active mind was often free to wander. He started to think about ways that he might improve his life. When he'd become successful, he remembered those thoughts.

"Work outside of school hours was necessary at an early age, and with such time as I had I turned towards interests of my own devising, making things, experimenting, and planning for the future," he said in his unpublished memoirs. "I had read of Edison and other successful inventors and the idea of making an invention appealed to me as one of the few available means to accomplish a change in one's economic status, while at the same time bringing to focus my interest in technical things and making it possible to make a contribution to society as well."

This "interest in technical things" soon focused on graphic arts and chemistry, both of which fascinated him. The printer he was working for gave him a small printing press that was going to be thrown away. While he was still in high school, Chet used the press to publish a little magazine for amateur chemists. "I don't think I printed two

Chester, with his mother, Ellen, and his father, Olaf, at Crestline, California in 1915.

Chester worked in a cement plant to earn money while he was in college.

issues," he remembered later, "and they weren't much. However, this experience did impress me with the difficulty of getting words into hard copy, and this started me thinking about duplicating processes. I started a little inventor's notebook, and I would jot down ideas from time to time."

Despite his financial difficulties, he graduated from high school in 1924. Shortly before he graduated, several students from the California Institute of Technology visited his high school. An excellent science student, Chet was interested in hearing about their experiences. Unfortunately, right after he graduated, there was simply no way he could attend the school, which was located in Pasadena, about a two-hour drive from his home.

But Chet Carlson was a determined young man. So he spent a year working to save some money, then enrolled in what was called a "cooperative program" at nearby Riverside Junior College. Students with little money would take classes for six weeks, then work for six weeks. If all went according to plan, they would complete two years of college work in four years.

But Chet showed his ability to go beyond conventional thinking by completing the work in three years. He took extra classes even though he was working even more hours in the laboratory of a cement plant to help support his father.

Then in the fall of 1928, he transferred to Caltech as a junior and earned his degree in physics on schedule in 1930, but he also had $1,400 worth of college debts to pay back because he had borrowed money to complete his education.

Unfortunately, his life was beset by example after example of terrible timing. Less than a year earlier, the Great Depression began when the stock market collapsed and jobs were virtually impossible to get. Shortly before getting his diploma, Carlson mailed letters to eighty-two companies, and got only one job offer. It was from Bell Labs on the East coast. He took the job and mailed money back to his father each week. Because he could no longer look after his father, he had a neighbor prepare meals for him each day until he died.

In 1944, the Battelle Institute provided Chester Carlson with $3,000 for research in exchange for a share of the profits that might be made from his photocopying process. Their share later turned out to be millions.

Chapter 3
Long Hours

The job Carlson finally found in New York was doing routine laboratory work for Bell Telephone Laboratories for $35 a week. That job was not to his liking, so he soon transferred to Bell's patent department. But as the Depression worsened, he was laid off. Fortunately, he was able to find a job with a patent attorney not long afterward, and after about a year in that position he moved over to a job with P.R. Mallory.

"By 1935 I was more or less settled," he told Alfred Dinsdale in an article that appeared in the *Journal of Photographic Science and Engineering* in 1963. "I had my job, but I didn't think I was getting ahead very fast. I was just living from hand to mouth, you might say, and I had just got married. It was kind of a hard struggle. So I thought the possibility of making an invention might kill two birds with one stone: it would be a chance to do the world some good and also a chance to do myself some good."

With all the boring hours he was putting in at work copying patent applications, the type of invention seemed obvious: Some kind of machine that would copy all those documents in a few seconds would save huge amounts of time.

Though most of his life so far hadn't been very lucky, he was fortunate in one respect. He lived in New York City, which has one of the world's largest and most complete libraries. He began spending nearly all the hours that he

Chester (right) as a young man. Even in his younger days, Chester kept an inventor's notebook where he jotted down ideas from time to time.

wasn't working inside the library, doing research on different types of imaging processes.

Very quickly he decided against anything using photography. The process involved messy chemicals. And he knew that many large corporations were investigating it. He didn't want to try to compete against them.

Soon he came across information about something called photoconductivity, a new field discovered by a Hungarian physicist named Paul Selenyi a few years earlier. When light strikes the surface of certain materials, its conductivity (the flow of electrons) increases. Carlson believed that if he could project the image of one of those patent documents onto a photoconductive surface, the electric current would flow only in the areas that the light hit. The areas that contained printing would be dark. No current would flow through them. That would create an electrically charged latent, or hidden, copy of the original document. Then "all" he had to do was transfer this latent copy to a piece of paper and he would have a copy of his patent document within just a small fraction of the time that it would take him to copy it by hand.

He began using his kitchen to conduct experiments, seeing how light affected different substances because he was convinced that his copying device would operate with light. One of the materials that demonstrated photoconductivity was sulfur. But one of sulfur's main characteristics is that it makes a terrible smell, especially when heated. After a series of unfortunate accidents—spilling sulfur all over the stove so that both he and his wife nearly passed out from the fumes, and having chemicals burst into flames—his wife Elsa was fed up.

So he moved his lab to a room in a building owned by his mother-in-law. She also rented part of this building to a hairdresser. It was above a tavern in Astoria in the New York borough of Queens. And as if his full-time job, long hours of research and constant experiments weren't enough, in 1936 he'd also begun taking classes at New York Law School at night to become a patent attorney so he could make more money. Not only that, he was in constant pain from arthritis of the spine that he'd recently contracted.

One thing, therefore, was very obvious: He needed help.

Chester Carlson's process of xerography was simple in theory but took years of hard work and millions of dollars before an accurate and inexpensive copy machine became a reality.

Chapter 4
Experiments

● ●

O tto Kornei, a German physicist who fled to the United States when Adolf Hitler came to power in his own country, had placed an ad in an electronics journal in hopes of finding work. Chet Carlson hired Otto and the two of them worked together, performing as many experiments as they could with the materials they could buy for $10 a month, which was all they could afford.

Carlson was convinced that if he could get dry particles to stick to a charged plate in a pattern corresponding to an image shining on the plate, he could make dry reproduction work. The basic idea was simple. Getting it to work was not so simple.

During the next several months, they had dozens and dozens of experiments that failed. Then came a fateful day.

"October, 22, 1938, was an historic occasion," Carlson said in Stephen Perkins' *The Manifesto of the Reprographic Revolution.* "I went to the lab that day and Otto had a freshly prepared sulfur coating on a zinc plate, we tried to see what we could do toward making a visible image. Otto took a glass microscope slide and printed on it in India ink the notation, '10-22-38 ASTORIA.'

"We pulled down the shade as dark as possible, then he rubbed the sulfur surface vigorously with a handkerchief to apply an electrostatic charge, laid the slide on the surface and placed the combination under a bright incandescent light for a few seconds. The slide was then removed and lycopodium powder sprinkled on the sulfur surface. By gently blowing on the surface, all the loose powder was removed and there was left on the surface a near-perfect duplicate in powder notation which had been printed on the glass slide.

"Both of us repeated the experiment several times to convince ourselves that it was true, then we made some permanent copies by transferring the powder images to wax paper and heating the sheets to melt the wax. Then we went to lunch to celebrate."

Carlson and Kornei had created the very first electrostatic copy. One of the very first copies of the legend "10-22-38 ASTORIA" was given to the Smithsonian Museum in 1985 and can now be seen there.

Soon afterward, Kornei was offered a job by IBM that paid much more and appeared to have far better prospects

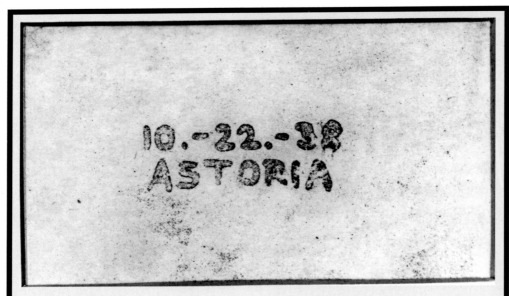

This is a reproduction of the first xerographic image that Carlson and Kornei made on October 22, 1938. It would be more than 20 years later before the first plain paper copier was ready for market.

than anything coming out of that cramped back room. So Carlson was back on his own. But he was certain that he had discovered the process that would be the foundation of his copying machine.

Carlson's process took five steps. First, a photoconductive plate was given an electrostatic charge (which is what gives you a shock when you walk on a rug and then touch a metal doorknob); this charge will only hold in the dark. Next, a printed page was placed close to the surface and light was shone on it; because of the light the charge held only in the places protected by the dark ink. The third step was dusting the surface with powdered ink, which stuck to the charged places. In the fourth step this image was transferred to a blank piece of paper. The final step was to apply heat to melt the ink so that it stuck to the paper.

Because of his experience working in a patent office, and his studies of patent law in night school, Carlson knew the importance of protecting his discovery, which he called "electrophotography." He'd applied for his first patent in 1937—even before he had made the process work successfully—because he was afraid that other would-be inventors might be doing the same research.

He didn't have to worry. The only notice the scientific world gave to Chester Carlson's first success appeared in a brief article in the *New York Times* on Friday, November 22, 1940. A science writer chanced upon the notice that the patent Carlson applied for three years earlier had been granted and wrote, "A new method of photography, in which the image is recorded electrically instead of chemically, and from which prints can be produced immediately without the usual development, is the subject of Patent 2,221,776, just granted to Chester F. Carlson of Jackson Heights, L.I." The article went on to describe the process and concluded by mentioning the many types of images that could be reproduced, adding that "the advantage would be that a permanent print could be obtained almost instantly."

Even before that article appeared, Carlson had tried to interest companies in developing his invention because he didn't have the financial resources to do it himself. From 1939 to 1944, he offered the rights to his process to every major office-equipment company. IBM, Remington Rand, RCA, General Electric—over 20 companies all turned him down. At that stage of development of the process there were still too many problems, such as blurry images and scorched, discolored paper, for the technicians to be able to see the possibilities in this process.

In addition, Carlson was again the victim of bad timing. It was now World War II. Few people were interested in a process that did not contribute directly to the war effort. No machinists could be spared from the factories to work on a machine that could put Carlson's process into action.

Not surprisingly, he sometimes gave up himself during these years, thinking that if no one anywhere was interested in his process, maybe it really wasn't important.

Those big companies weren't the only ones who turned him down. His wife Elsa was tired of all the hours he spent on his job and on his research that didn't seem to be going anywhere. So Chester and Elsa divorced. Several years later, he married a woman named Dorris Hudgins. They remained together until his death.

But in the meantime, his faith in his process finally began to be rewarded. Russell Dayton of the Battelle Memorial Institute, a nonprofit industrial research organization in Columbus, Ohio, dropped by the Mallory Company in 1944 to discuss a patent application. There he met Carlson, who by then had received his law degree and been promoted to head of the patent department.

During the course of their conversation, Carlson mentioned his invention. He showed Dayton samples of the copies he'd made. Dayton was interested, and that chance meeting soon led to a royalty-sharing agreement between the Battelle Institute and Carlson. Battelle would provide $3,000 worth of research in exchange for a share of any profits that were made. Carlson may have thought his troubles were over. But if he did, he was wrong again.

Improving the process was one thing. Developing the process into a working machine, and then making enough of those machines to show a profit, was something entirely different. It would require money—lots of money. Far more money than either he or Battelle had. And the patience to keep spending money before a single successful copy machine was produced.

Before his process, so beautifully simple in theory, could become the practical reality of a quick, easy, accurate, and inexpensive method of copying documents, Chester Carlson needed someone who was as obsessed as he was. Someone who would devote not only years of hard work but lots and lots of money to making the process work. Soon he would meet that person.

Joe Wilson (CEO of Xerox from 1946-1966) with the first production models of the Xerox 914 copier. Joe had the vision to see what Chester Carlson's patent could do for the Haloid Company. It was his support that kept the Haloid Company pushing forward through years of frustration.

Chapter 5

Joe Wilson

● ●

In 1906, the same year that Chester Carlson was born in Seattle, four businessmen in Rochester, New York founded the Haloid Company. The company, which made photographic paper in a small shop located above a shoe factory, took its name from the haloid salts used in the coating of the paper. One of the four businessmen was Rochester mayor Joseph C. Wilson. Four years later his son, Joe Wilson, was born.

Young Joe had a completely different childhood than Chet Carlson. While Chet was living in poverty, working hard, and moving frequently with his ailing parents, Joe was growing up in comfort and security in his well-established family in Rochester.

Somewhat reluctantly—he had graduated from Harvard Business School and had big ambitions—Joe Wilson took his father's place as president of the Haloid Company in 1946. The company's future did not look good. The Second World War had just ended, and so had the company's main source of business, wartime orders from the U.S. Government for photographic paper. It was clear that if the company was going to survive, much less grow and prosper, it needed new products. Joe Wilson asked John Dessauer, his chief of research, to keep informed about new patents and read a wide variety of technical publications. If he could find a promising invention to nurture and introduce into the marketplace, his company could become larger and more profitable.

Chester Carlson and Joe Wilson were looking for each other. Carlson had been looking in all the wrong places—trying to interest the big, powerful, successful corporations in his process. Joe Wilson, who knew a lot more about business than Carlson did or wanted to, was looking in the right places.

Meanwhile, the Battelle Institute was making some progress with Carlson's process. The staff at Battelle developed a new photoconductive plate covered with selenium, which was much better than the sulfur Carlson had used. They also spent nearly a year developing a corona wire that would both apply a uniform electrostatic charge to the plate and transfer the powder from the plate to the paper.

Their most important contribution was the invention of better dry ink, which was called "toner." Carlson's use of lycopodium powder, or moss spores, didn't work very well because it produced a fuzzy image. The toner developed at Battelle was fine iron powder mixed with the salt ammonium chloride and a type of plastic. The ammonium chloride provided a sharper image because it had the same charge as the metal plate. In the areas where there was no image, the iron particles stuck to the salt and not to the plate. The plastic material melted when heated and fused the iron particles to the paper.

In 1945, Dessauer noticed an abstract on the electrophotography process invented by Chester Carlson. He showed it to Joe Wilson and the two of them went to Columbus to visit the Battelle Institute to see the process. Once he saw the demonstration given by Chester Carlson and the team at Battelle, Joe Wilson was interested. Very interested. He thought that if this process could be developed into a product that made reasonably priced copies it could be a good seller.

Wilson went back to Rochester and like the good businessman he was, began doing a little research. He investigated the patents. He read about photographic processes. He found out about other devices that were being used to make copies. Everything he learned convinced him that this shy quiet man, Chester Carlson, had discovered something enormously important. But not even he had an idea at this time how important Carlson's process actually would become.

On January 2, 1947 Haloid and Battelle signed an agreement giving Haloid rights to manufacture products based on Carlson's process in exchange for royalties. It also obligated Haloid to share the costs of development. Many years later, Wilson said about his decision, "I would have to be psychoanalyzed to say if I would take the same risk again. It's when you're very young and naïve that you have the courage to make the right decisions."

The Haloid Company in the 1940s

Peter McColough was the man who would eventually succeed
Joe Wilson as the company president.

Chapter 6

The Haloid Company

• •

People at Haloid didn't think "electrophotography" sounded very exciting, so they suggested finding a new name for Carlson's process. A professor at Ohio State University, near where Battelle was located, suggested combining two words from classical Greek: "xeros," which meant dry and "graphein," which meant writing, to make the word "xerography."

Now Battelle, Haloid, and Carlson had a name for the process, but developing a machine to produce the "dry writing" the process called for continued to stump them. They kept running into technical difficulties. The costs of development were enormous: between 1947 and 1960 Haloid spent about $75 million on the xerographic process, which was more than the company earned in that period. They kept borrowing more and more money, and issuing new shares of stock. Wilson and other company executives accepted their pay in stock. Some even mortgaged their homes to put still more money into the company.

Although Joe Wilson several times offered Chester Carlson a position at Haloid, Carlson refused. He just wasn't comfortable working as part of a team. He preferred being an adviser and consultant, even though he moved to Rochester in 1948 to help with the development of xerography. While Chester Carlson was never officially employed by Haloid, he developed a respect and a working rapport with the researchers there that enabled them all to survive a dozen years of struggle with disappointment after disappointment and failure after failure.

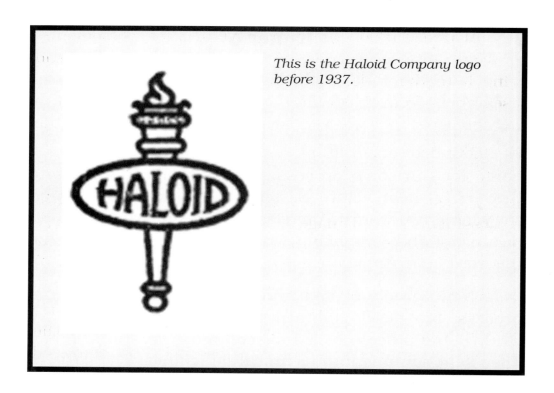

This is the Haloid Company logo before 1937.

Peter McColough, the man who Joe Wilson eventually picked to succeed him as company president, shared his memories of Chester Carlson with interviewers.

"Carlson was a very quiet, private, very, very humble man. He had no airs about him. I remember when I used to go see him; he had an office in a laboratory. I was quite young. He didn't have a title. Obviously, he was a very senior person. He would be sort of apologizing for taking my time. I was thinking just the reverse, I was taking his time. He was a thoroughly delightful guy, but very modest, very shy. I'm not sure that a lot of people understand that he really played no role, it was at his request, in the management of the company. He had a lot of influence in the company in terms of the development of xerography, suggestions in the technical area, but he was not a businessman."

At first Carlson was protective of his developments. He would mix the carrier for toner in his basement and bring it to the Haloid labs in soda bottles. One of the researchers from that time remembered that "We used to joke that the recipe was two bottles of ginger ale and a bottle of 7-Up. That's how Chet would bring the stuff to us."

On October 22, 1948, exactly ten years to the day after Chester Carlson and Otto Kornei made the first successful dry copied image of "10-22-38 ASTORIA," Battelle and Haloid demonstrated the Carlson process at a meeting of the Optical Society of America in Detroit. Another demonstration was given the same week for the publishing industry at the Waldorf-Astoria in Manhattan. Nearly everyone who saw the demonstrations agreed that the process was interesting, but they seemed a bit confused about its possible future.

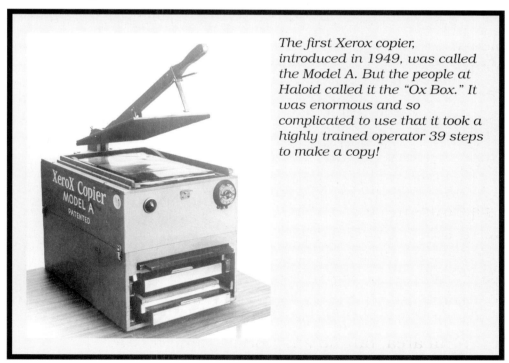

The first Xerox copier, introduced in 1949, was called the Model A. But the people at Haloid called it the "Ox Box." It was enormous and so complicated to use that it took a highly trained operator 39 steps to make a copy!

The first xerographic copier, introduced in 1949, was officially known as the Model A, but the people around Haloid called it the Ox Box. It was enormous and was made up of three separate machines. It was not automatic. In fact it was so complicated to operate that even a very highly trained operator took 39 steps to make a single copy. The process required two or three minutes and the operator had to carry a heavy plate from one machine to the next.

A few of these Model A copiers were sold and shipped out, but they came back almost immediately. The businesses that tried them found they were too complicated to use. That disaster of a first attempt might have put the Haloid Company out of business. But by a lucky accident, it turned out that the Ox Box, although it wasn't much use as a copier, was a good way to make the paper masters for offset printing presses. Enough of the Model A machines were sold for that purpose to keep the company going. It also provided some money for Carlson, though nowhere near what he would eventually receive.

Over the next ten years, the Haloid Company tried a few other xerographic devices: the Foto-Flo Model C Photo-Copying Machine, the Xerox Lith-Master, and the Copyflo. None of them did any better than the Ox Box. They were also awkward and complicated. Other companies were also trying to develop products that would produce inexpensive copies for office use. In 1950 the 3M Company introduced the Thermo-Fax, which used infrared heat to create images on special paper. In 1952 American Photocopy brought out the Dial-A-Matic Autostat, which used a photographic process. In 1953 Kodak's Verifax appeared, using chemical developers.

These other copying techniques had serious drawbacks. All of them required special paper that had to be purchased from the manufacturer. The two that were based on techniques of photography—the Autostat and the Verifax—produced damp copies that had to dry before they could be used, and smelled bad besides. The Thermo-fax copies were so sensitive to heat that they kept getting darker and darker until they were impossible to read.

Meanwhile the Haloid Company kept plugging away. They tried to recruit talented young people to help them develop xerography. Some of the people they interviewed were scared off by the obviously raggedy surroundings— vice presidents had bookshelves made out of orange crates and carried lunchboxes. The new employees were told that their first task would be building themselves a desk, although a chair would be provided. Still, there were enough talented people who were inspired by the belief that Chester Carlson and Joe Wilson had in this process that the company continued to struggle along, even though the technical problems they were grappling with seemed unending.

At one point Haloid did get so discouraged that they thought about selling their xerography rights to IBM. But IBM wasn't very interested, and nothing came of it. In 1955 Haloid got full title to Chester Carlson's patents in exchange for 50,000 shares of Haloid stock. That was the deal that would eventually make Carlson a multi-millionaire. But there was still a long hard road to travel before then.

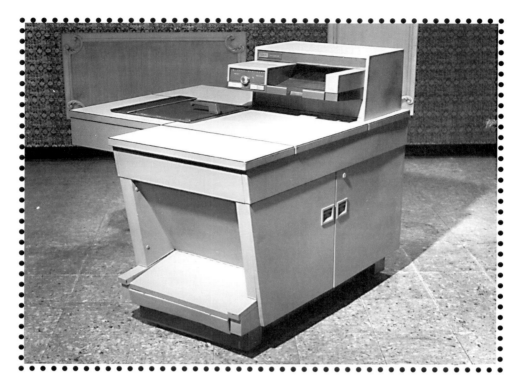

The Xerox Model 914, introduced in 1959, was the machine that would make the Xerox Company and Chester Carlson millions of dollars. It was the first automatic, plain paper copier. Though it was a challenge getting it to work properly, the idea of selling copies instead of the copiers worked wonders for the company that had invested so heavily in the technology.

Chapter 7
Model 914

∙∙

The machine that would eventually create the multi-billion dollar photocopying industry was known as the 914, because it could copy sheets of paper up to 9x14 inches. But it developed a seemingly endless series of problems. One problem was that the paper would stick to the glass plate because of the static electricity. One of the Haloid engineers was in his garage pumping up a tire when the solution to that problem occurred to him. He put a piece of paper on the hood of his car and blew air at it with the bicycle pump. The paper flew. He thought that putting little air nozzles in the copying machines would move the paper along—and it did.

Another problem was how to get rid of the excess toner. The engineers decided to use rotating fur brushes, but had to do dozens of experiments before they found the best kind of fur to use, which turned out to be from Australian rabbits.

But a much more serious problem was the habit the 914 had of bursting into flames. When the copy paper jammed—because the puff of air that was supposed to move it along didn't—the paper might brush against the hot rollers that were used to fuse the ink. The sheet of paper would then catch fire and smoke would billow out of the machine. This was obviously not a strong selling point for the machine, so the engineers came up with the idea of attaching a fire extinguisher to the copier. The people in the marketing department did not think this was a good idea. How could they sell a product that had to have its own fire extinguisher?

The two departments finally arrived at a compromise: the engineers would attach the fire extinguishers to the copiers, but they would call them "scorch eliminators."

At one point, the chief engineer at Haloid saw Carlson in a hallway. Carlson was struggling to get one of the early models of the 914 to work, without success. The engineer tried to help him, and he couldn't get the copier to work either. At that point Carlson said, "We better walk away from here right now. You're the chief engineer on the machine and I'm the inventor. If people see even we can't get the thing working, they're going to think we're headed for disaster."

The engineers at Haloid worked 24 hours a day during 1957 and 1958 to develop the 914. Because the company couldn't afford to heat the building at night, they worked in parkas, boots, and mittens through the cold upper New York winters. Finally they were ready. They had a product they were ready to manufacture. But that was another problem. They were seriously broke. For twelve years they had been spending more money developing the xerography process than the Haloid Company had made.

Once again they approached IBM with a proposal to manufacture the copier as a joint venture. IBM executives studied the proposal, but decided that there wouldn't be a market for more than 5000 of the machines. There just wasn't enough profit in making so few. So they passed.

Haloid went ahead by itself. In 1959 the first production model of the new 914 came off the assembly line. It weighed about 650 pounds and was bigger than a large desk.

Not long before, Joe Wilson and Sol Linowitz had been taking a Sunday morning walk together to talk about the name they should use for a trademark. As they discussed the problem, they looked up and saw a billboard advertising Kodak, the camera and film company, which was also located in Rochester. They both had the same idea at once: use the same letter to begin and end the word. So they took the beginning of xerography and simply added another "x" at the end. At first people thought that "XeroX" (which was originally spelled with a capital X at the beginning and end) was an odd sort of word, something like a new flu remedy. But it wouldn't be long before the entire world would recognize the word.

The company quickly changed its name to Haloid Xerox. (In 1961 it would be changed again, to the Xerox Corporation). In the autumn the chairman of the board put the first document in the 914 copier to demonstrate it to the company's sales force. He pushed the button. When the paper came out, he held it up. It was blank. Someone lifted

The new Haloid Xerox Company logo in 1957.

The Xerox 914 product team gathered in 1985 as the Model 914 was being readied for presentation to the Smithsonian.

the cover and smiled—the chairman had put the document in with the wrong side down. He turned it over, pushed the button again, and this time a perfect copy came out.

When the 914 was presented to the public on September 16, 1959, at the Sherry-Netherland Hotel in New York City, two copiers were demonstrated. One caught fire, nearly causing the vice president who was operating it to have a stroke. The other one, however, worked perfectly. *Business Week* magazine put the Model 914 Xerox Copier on the cover.

There were still some problems. The 914 was extremely expensive and very large. The salesmen could hardly carry it around to demonstrate to customers, and even if they had been able to, how many customers would pay thousands of dollars for a copier? The solutions to these problems proved that genius at Haloid Xerox Company was not restricted to the engineers and physicists. The marketing department proved capable of genius as well.

Chester Carlson (middle) never worked for the Haloid Company. He turned down several offers of employment, preferring to work on his inventions at his own pace. It was the 1960s before he realized any considerable profit from his patent and before he died, he gave most of his money away. In this photograph, he is seen with Joe Wilson and Dr. John Dessauer demonstrating an early xerographic printer.

Chapter 8
Multimillionaire

●●

P eter McColough had been promoted to be the general manager of sales for Haloid Xerox in 1959. He was faced with the problem of selling a machine that cost four thousand dollars to produce—and would have to sell for much more than that once all the other costs of marketing, advertising, and administration were figured in. It was a machine too large to take to businesses to demonstrate. It was also a machine that had followed a string of previous failures. McColough was afraid that no one would buy it. So he came up with the brilliant idea of selling copies rather than copying machines.

The company attached meters to the 914, charged a low monthly rent that allowed the user to make up to 2,000 copies, and charged four cents for each additional copy. They also allowed customers to return the machines within fifteen days if they weren't satisfied. Another device the marketing people used was to place the Xerox 914 in heavily traveled public places where lots of people would see it.

The advertising department created ads for television emphasizing how easy the 914 was to use. In the first ad shown, a man asks his little daughter to make a copy for him, and the child does it easily (and then makes a copy of her doll). When the girl takes the copy back to her father, he asks which one is the original. Neither of them can tell. Competitors were so upset about this commercial that they accused Xerox of using a midget and not a real child.

Another ad wasn't as effective. In this one a monkey was trained to make a copy. Unfortunately, although the commercial did show how easy it was to operate the machine, men in offices left bananas on the machines for the secretaries who did the copying, and the ladies were not happy. The ad was quickly cancelled.

The original estimate was that each machine might make 10,000 copies a month. The actual average turned out to be 40,000 copies per month. The copies were so good that people began making copies of copies as well as of original documents. It didn't take long for companies to realize that the Xerox 914 copier was a machine that was just as vital to their success as typewriters and telephones. Soon the demand to buy the machines—not just rent them— was so great that the company had to scramble to keep up. For a while a new series of production problems was created by the rapid growth that no one could have predicted. But the company eventually solved all those difficulties, and the Xerox Corporation became one of the greatest success stories in the history of American business.

Ten years previously, in 1955, The Battelle Institute and Haloid had signed an agreement changing their agreement from being based on royalties to having Battelle paid in cash and stock in the Xerox Company. By 1966, Battelle had received over five million dollars and 355,000 shares of Xerox stock. According to their original agreement, Chester Carlson's share was 40%. With the astounding success of the 914 copier, Xerox stock went up in value. Way up. Way way up.

After a lifetime of economic difficulty—from a childhood of poverty, through a young adulthood in the midst of the

The Battelle Institute was a nonprofit company that helped with the research for Chester Carlson's "xerography." Chester and Battelle had an agreement to share royalties.

Great Depression, to mature years of constant struggle during which what money he made was invested in further development of his xerographic process—Chester Carlson was quite suddenly rich. Very rich. About $200 million dollars worth of rich.

McColough, who became the president of Xerox Corporation after Wilson retired, recalls the impact that wealth had on Chester Carlson in the book *Xerox, American Samurai*: "I think the amount of money he eventually made became much greater than he thought. I had some discussions with him about this. The money didn't come until later in his life and I think the amount of money that he made was a great burden to him. He used to talk about the many millions he made, about the responsibility of using that money wisely. How he could give it away wisely. I had the impression that he might have been a happier man if he had made two million bucks instead of more than $200 million."

McColough thought that Carlson was the wealthiest inventor of all time. Unlike people who were businessmen as well as inventors, like Henry Ford, and who made their money manufacturing a product based on their own invention, "Chester had nothing to do with that. In terms just of a guy making an invention or several inventions and reaping the rewards of inventions alone, Chester Carlson is probably the wealthiest inventor of all time."

A year before his death his wife asked him if he had any unfulfilled desires.

"Just one," he said. "I would like to die a poor man."

When he died he had given away more than $150 million. U Thant, secretary-general of the United Nations at that time, sent this tribute to Carlson's memorial service in honor of his substantial financial contributions: "His concern for the future of the human situation was genuine, and his dedication to the principles of the United Nations was profound."

Because Chester Carlson guarded his privacy so carefully, there is no way of knowing all of the charities and organizations he gave his money to. In many instances he gave the large donations anonymously so that even the organizations themselves did not know where the money came from.

Carlson died suddenly in 1968 at the age of 62. He was walking down 57th Street near 5th Avenue in New York, on his way to see a movie, when he had a heart attack. It must have seemed to the other people walking on that street

Xerox Square in Rochester, New York

Anne Mulcahy was appointed president and chief executive officer of Xerox Corporation in July 2001, making her one of only five female CEOs of a Fortune 500 company at that time.

Dorris and Chester Carlson in 1967, about a year before Chester died.

that he was an ordinary man, and he was, really. He had never wanted or expected power in the business world or great wealth. He certainly never expected that he would create a process that would completely revolutionize business practices and would be the basis of one of the most successful worldwide corporations ever developed. It also founded a vast copying industry that generates billions of dollars every year, with machines ranging from tiny desktop models in private homes to big machines that can print hundreds of copies per minute and even put them together in numerical order.

All Chester Carlson had wanted was a way to make good clear copies quickly and inexpensively. But he wanted it with a stubbornness and dedication that truly was extraordinary.

Chester Carlson Chronology

- **1906** born on February 8 in Seattle, Washington
- **1923** mother dies
- **1924** graduates from high school in San Bernardino, California
- **1925** attends junior college in Riverside, California
- **1930** receives B.S. degree in physics from California Institute of Technology; begins work for Bell Labs but is laid off because of Depression
- **1934** employed by P.R. Mallory, an electronics firm, in their patent department
- **1935** studies patent law in night classes at New York Law School
- **1937** applies for first patent for process of electrophotography
- **1938** with assistant Otto Kornei, makes first successful xerographic reproduction
- **1939** receives law degree from New York Law School
- **1940** passes bar exam and becomes a patent lawyer in New York State
- **1944** signs royalty-sharing deal with the Battelle Institute in exchange for $3,000 in research funds
- **1947** signs licensing agreement with Haloid Company, which later changes its name to Xerox Corporation
- **1949** introduces Model A copier using the xerography process
- **1959** introduces Xerox 914 copier, the first successful dry copier using plain paper
- **1964** named Inventor of the Year by the Patent, Trademark & Copyright Research Institute
- **1965** becomes multi-millionaire worth $200 million; donates most of fortune to charities
- **1968** dies of a heart attack on September 19th
- **1988** US postage stamp in the "Great Americans" series honoring Chester Carlson is issued

The Copy Machine Timeline

- **100 BC** Chinese begin making copies of inscriptions on stone tablets by rubbing ink and absorbent paper on the tablets.
- **105 BC** paper invented in China; made from hemp, bark, and used fish nets.
- **11th century** Chinese invent movable type.

- **1454** Johannes Gutenberg publishes Bible.
- **1476** William Caxton establishes England's first printing press.
- **1604** printing of King James Bible.
- **1609** *Avisa Relation oder Zeitung*, the world's first newspaper, is printed in Germany.
- **1640** Bay Psalm Book is first book printed in American colonies.
- **1725** Johann Heinrich Schulze discovers that light produces faint darkened images on mixtures of chalk and silver nitrate.
- **1802** Thomas Wedgwood uses silver nitrate to produce silhouettes but cannot "fix" the images.
- **1806** carbon paper invented.
- **1819** Sir John Herschel discovers photographic fixative, hyposulfite of soda, which makes permanent images.
- **1822** Dr. William Church develops first mechanical typesetting device.
- **1827** Joseph Niépce produces first successful photographic picture, using material that hardens on exposure to light. It requires an exposure of eight hours.
- **1837** Louis Daguerre discovers method of developing photographic plates, which greatly reduces exposure time from eight hours to half an hour. Resulting images are called Daguerreotypes.
- **1839** Sir John Herschel invents word "photography," using Greek words for light and writing.
- **1842** ferric-salt blueprinting process is invented.
- **1863** American William Bullock develops web-fed newspaper press, which uses continuous rolls of paper instead of printing one sheet at a time.
- **1884** George Eastman introduces flexible film.
- **1887** A.B. Dick Company begins producing mimeograph machine following its invention by Thomas Edison.
- **1888** George Eastman introduces box camera, also known as Kodak Camera, which makes photography accessible to most people.
- **1909** photostat process is used to make copies, using photographic paper rather than film. Copies are negative (white text on black background).
- **1938** Chester Carlson invents xerography.
- **1953** invention of carbonless paper, used primarily for business forms.
- **1959** Haloid Xerox introduces Model 914, first fully automatic photocopier.
- **1963** Polaroid Corporation introduces instant color print film.
- **1968** 3M Corporation introduces first full-color copier.
- **1975** IBM Corporation produces first laser printer.

- **1984** Hewlett-Packard Corporation produces first desktop laser printer, the LaserJet.
- **1985** first xerographic copy "10-22-38 ASTORIA" and the 914 copier presented to the Smithsonian Museum.

For Further Reading

Books

Bailey, Joseph H. *Xerographic Copier: Small Inventions That Make a Big Difference*. Washington DC: National Geographic Society, 1984.

Flatow, Ira. *They All Laughed*. New York: Harper Collins Publishers, 1992.

Jacobson, Gary and John Hillkirk. *Xerox: American Samurai*. New York: Macmillan Publishing Co., 1986.

Kearns, David T. and David A. Nadler. *Prophets in the Dark*. New York: Harper Collins Publishing, 1992

Lomask, Milton. *Inventions and Technology: Great Lives*. New York: Macmillan Publishing Co., 1995.

—. *Marshall Cavendish Library of Science: Technology*. Long Island, NY: Marshall Cavendish Corp., 1989

Articles

Caney, Steven. "The Invention of the Xerox Machine," in *Steven Caney's Invention Book*. New York: Workman Publishing Co., Inc. 1985.

DeSimone, Daniel V. "Invention, the First Step, Is Often Most Difficult." *New York Times*. January 8, 1968, pg. 138, col. 1.

Dinsdale, Alfred. "Chester F. Carlson, Inventor of Xerography—A Biography." *The Journal of Photographic Science and Engineering*, vol. 7, 1963, pp. 1-4.

Hall, Dennis G. And Rita M. "Chester F. Carlson: A Man to Remember." *Optics and Photonics News*, September, 2000, pp. 14-18.

Jones, Stacy V. "Xerography Inventor Is Honored." *New York Times*. May 8, 1965, p. 35, col. 2.

Schnittrott, et. al., eds. "Xerography" in *Eureka*. Vol. 5. New York: U.X.L., 1995

Primary Sources

The complete papers, inventions, notebooks, and correspondence of Chester F. Carlson are housed at the New York Public Library. Copies are in the Rochester Institute of Technology and the University of Rochester.

On the Web:

Chester F. Carlson Biography
http://www.lib.rochester.edu/car/ChesterCarlson/carlsonbio.htm
Chester F. Carlson, Electrophotography
http://www.invent.org/book-text/20.html
Chester Floyd Carlson
http://www.northstar.k12.ak.us/schools/ryn/projects/inventors/carlson
Perkins, Stephen. The Manifesto of the Reprographic Revolution.
http://www.the914.com/xerographicore.htm
Xerography
http://members.tripod.com/~earthdude1/xerox/index.html"
Xerox
http://www.dromo.com/fusionanomaly/xerox.html

Glossary

· ·

corona wire - wire in a Xerox copier that transfers the electrical charge to the plate and also causes the toner to stick to the paper

electrophotography - first term given to the process which later became known as xerography.

haloid salt - substance used in the coating of conventional photographic paper

lycopodium powder - moss spores, one of the earliest substances used to create an image in xerography.

offset printing - printing process in which a zinc or aluminum plate is treated chemically to hold ink to reproduce an image.

photoconductivity - ability of certain materials to alter their ability to conduct electricity when exposed to light.

royalties - monies paid to the owner of a patent or copyright for using the process or ideas in a commercial product.

selenium - photoconductive material used by the Battelle Institute to replace the sulfur originally used by Chester Carlson in his xerographic process

toner - dry ink used in xerography, composed of iron particles, aluminum chloride, and plastic material.

Verifax - copying machine using photographic chemicals and producing damp copies, brought out by Kodak.

xerography - from Greek words meaning "dry writing," a process developed by Chester Carlson using the principle of photoconductivity to make instant copies on plain paper.

Index